Unlocking Your Potential: Self-Coaching for Success in Business Leadership

Jeffrey Yeomans

Contents

Chapter 1: Introduction to Self-Coaching for Success in Business Leadership

Understanding the Power of Self-Coaching

In today's fast-paced and competitive business world, self-coaching has emerged as a powerful tool for business leaders to unlock their potential and achieve success in their professional lives. Many successful leaders have credited self-coaching as a crucial component in their journey towards goal setting and achievement. This section aims to provide business leaders with a comprehensive understanding of the power of self-coaching, emphasizing its significance in setting and reaching their goals.

Self-coaching is a process that involves introspection, self-reflection, and self-analysis. It enables business leaders to examine their strengths, weaknesses, motivations, and aspirations. By taking charge of their own growth and development, leaders can identify areas for improvement and devise strategies to overcome obstacles that hinder their progress.

One of the key aspects of self-coaching is goal setting. Setting clear and meaningful goals is vital for business leaders to stay focused, motivated, and driven towards success. Self-coaching empowers leaders to define their goals with clarity, align them with their personal values and aspirations, and break them down into manageable action steps. This process helps leaders gain a sense of direction, prioritize their efforts, and stay on track amidst the chaos of the business world.

Self-coaching also enables business leaders to develop a growth mindset, which is essential for continuous learning and development. By adopting a growth mindset, leaders embrace challenges, view failures as opportunities for growth, and seek out new knowledge and skills. Through self-coaching, leaders can identify areas where they need to learn and improve, and then seek out resources, mentors, or training programs to enhance their skills and knowledge base.

Furthermore, self-coaching enhances self-awareness, which is crucial for effective leadership. By gaining a deeper understanding of their emotions, thoughts, and behaviors, leaders can better manage themselves and their relationships with others. Self-coaching helps leaders identify their triggers, manage stress, and build resilience, enabling them to navigate challenging situations with confidence and composure.

In conclusion, self-coaching holds immense power for business leaders seeking to set and achieve their goals. By engaging in self-reflection, goal setting, and personal growth, leaders can unlock their potential and become more effective in their roles. The power of self-coaching lies in its ability to empower leaders to take control of their own development, enhance self-awareness, and cultivate a growth mindset. As business leaders embrace self-coaching, they position themselves for greater success, not only in their professional lives but also in their personal lives.

Benefits of Self-Coaching for Business Leaders

In today's fast-paced business world, effective leadership is crucial for success. As a business leader, you are constantly faced with challenges, decisions, and the responsibility of guiding your team towards achieving goals. To navigate these complexities and unlock your true potential as a leader, self-coaching can be a powerful tool.

Self-coaching for goal setting and achievement is a niche within the leadership development field that focuses on empowering individuals to take charge of their own growth and development. It involves utilizing a range of strategies, techniques, and tools to enhance self-awareness, set meaningful goals, and develop the skills and mindset necessary for success.

One of the key benefits of self-coaching is the ability to gain greater clarity and focus. By taking the time to reflect on your strengths, weaknesses, and areas for improvement, you can identify specific goals that align with your vision and values. This clarity enables you to prioritize your actions, make better decisions, and allocate resources effectively.

Self-coaching also fosters a sense of self-accountability. As a leader, it is essential to hold yourself responsible for your own growth and development. By actively engaging in the self-coaching process, you establish a framework for continuous improvement. This self-accountability not only drives personal growth but also sets a positive example for your team, inspiring them to take ownership of their own development as well.

Furthermore, self-coaching empowers you to develop the skills and mindset required to overcome challenges and achieve your goals. Through self-reflection, goal setting, and action planning, you can identify and address any limiting beliefs or self-doubt that may be holding you back. By building self-confidence, resilience, and a growth mindset, you become better equipped to navigate obstacles, adapt to change, and drive innovation within your organization.

Another significant benefit of self-coaching is the flexibility it offers. Unlike traditional coaching, which often involves scheduling sessions with external coaches, self-coaching allows you to take charge of your development at your own pace and in your own time. This flexibility ensures that you can integrate self-coaching seamlessly into your busy schedule, making it a sustainable and ongoing practice.

In conclusion, self-coaching for business leaders is a powerful approach to unlocking your potential and achieving success. By gaining clarity and focus, fostering self-accountability, developing essential skills and mindset, and enjoying the flexibility it offers, you can become a more effective leader, inspire your team, and drive your organization towards its goals. Embrace the benefits of self-coaching and unlock your true leadership potential.

Overcoming Challenges in Business Leadership through Self-Coaching

In the fast-paced and ever-evolving world of business leadership, challenges are inevitable. From managing teams to making critical decisions, the role of a business leader requires constant adaptation and growth. However, the question arises - how can one effectively overcome these challenges and continue to succeed in their leadership journey? The answer lies in the power of self-coaching.

Self-coaching for goal setting and achievement has emerged as a powerful tool for business leaders. By taking charge of their own personal development and growth, leaders can navigate through obstacles, strengthen their skills, and unlock their full potential. This section explores the art of self-coaching and its significance in overcoming challenges in business leadership.

One of the primary challenges faced by business leaders is the ability to set and achieve goals effectively. Self-coaching provides a systematic approach to goal setting, enabling leaders to define their objectives, outline strategies, and track progress. Through self-reflection and introspection, leaders can identify their strengths and weaknesses, enabling them to leverage their strengths and work on areas that require improvement. By becoming their own coach, leaders can develop an unobstructed vision and align their actions towards achieving their goals.

Another common challenge in business leadership is decision-making. The pressure of making the right choices can be overwhelming, and the fear of failure can hinder progress. Self-coaching equips leaders with the skills to overcome these challenges by cultivating self-awareness and emotional intelligence. Through self-reflection and self-analysis, leaders can identify biases, manage emotions, and make well-informed decisions. Self-coaching also encourages leaders to seek feedback from trusted sources, fostering a culture of continuous learning and improvement.

Furthermore, self-coaching helps leaders develop resilience in the face of adversity. Business leadership often involves managing crises, managing conflicts, and navigating through uncertain situations. By adopting a self-coaching mindset, leaders can cultivate a growth mindset, embrace challenges as opportunities for growth, and develop the resilience needed to bounce back from setbacks.

In conclusion, self-coaching is a powerful tool that enables business leaders to overcome challenges and unlock their potential. By embracing self-coaching for goal setting and achievement, leaders can enhance their decision-making abilities, develop resilience, and navigate through the complexities of business leadership with confidence. By becoming their own coach, leaders can truly unlock their potential and achieve success in their leadership journey.

Chapter 2: Setting Goals for Business Success

The Importance of Goal Setting in Business Leadership

In today's competitive business landscape, effective leadership is crucial for success. As a business leader, you are responsible for guiding your team towards achieving the organization's objectives. However, to truly unlock your potential as a leader, it is essential to understand and implement the power of goal setting.

Goal setting provides direction and purpose, both on an individual and organizational level. By setting clear and measurable goals, you create a roadmap that helps you stay focused and motivated. Without goals, you may find yourself wandering aimlessly, lacking the drive and direction necessary to succeed.

Setting goals also allows you to prioritize tasks and allocate resources efficiently. As a leader, you have limited time and resources at your disposal. By identifying the most important goals, you can ensure that your team's efforts are aligned with the overall vision of the organization. This not only increases productivity but also enhances the chances of achieving business objectives.

Moreover, goal setting promotes accountability and encourages personal growth. When goals are established, individuals understand what is expected of them and can take ownership of their responsibilities. This fosters a sense of accountability, as team members strive to accomplish their targets and contribute to the collective success. Additionally, setting challenging yet attainable goals pushes individuals out of their comfort zones, leading to continuous improvement and development.

Self-coaching plays a vital role in the goal-setting process. As a business leader, self-coaching allows you to reflect on your strengths and weaknesses, identify areas for improvement, and establish personal goals that align with the organization's objectives. By taking control of your own development, you become a role model for your team, inspiring them to take charge of their own growth.

To effectively self-coach for goal setting and achievement, it is important to establish a systematic approach. Start by clearly defining your long-term vision and then break it down into smaller, actionable goals. Ensure that these goals are specific, measurable, attainable, relevant, and time-bound (SMART). Regularly review and track your progress, adjusting your actions as needed.

In conclusion, goal setting is the cornerstone of effective business leadership. By setting clear goals, you provide direction, enhance productivity, foster accountability, and promote personal growth. Embracing self-coaching for goal setting and achievement empowers you to take control of your own development and inspires your team to do the same. Remember, unlocking your potential as a leader begins with unlocking the power of goal setting.

Defining Clear and Measurable Goals

In the quest for success, setting clear and measurable goals is an essential step. Without a clear destination in mind, it is easy to get lost along the way and lose sight of what you genuinely want to achieve. In this section, we will delve into the importance of defining clear and measurable goals and how it can propel business leaders towards success.

First, clear goals provide a sense of direction. They function as a roadmap that guides business leaders towards their desired outcomes. By clearly defining what you want to achieve, you can identify the steps necessary to reach your goals. This clarity ensures that your efforts are focused, efficient, and purposeful.

Furthermore, measurable goals enable business leaders to gauge their progress and track their achievements. When goals are measurable, it becomes easier to determine if you are on the right track or if adjustments need to be made. Measuring progress helps maintain motivation and provides a sense of accomplishment as milestones are reached.

Moreover, clear, and measurable goals promote accountability. When goals are not clearly defined, it becomes difficult to hold oneself accountable for their achievement. However, when goals are specific and measurable, it becomes easier to assess performance and take responsibility for the results. This accountability fosters a sense of ownership and drives business leaders to take the necessary actions to achieve their goals.

In the realm of self-coaching for goal setting and achievement, defining clear and measurable goals is crucial. It allows business leaders to take control of their own development and progress towards their desired outcomes. Through self-coaching, leaders can identify their strengths and weaknesses, set realistic and challenging goals, and develop action plans to achieve them.

To unlock your potential as a business leader, it is imperative to define clear and measurable goals. By doing so, you can gain clarity, track progress, and cultivate accountability. Investing time and effort into setting goals that are specific and measurable will undoubtedly lead to greater success in business leadership. So, take the plunge, define your goals, and unlock your potential for self-coaching and achievement in the business world.

Creating an Action Plan for Goal Achievement

As business leaders, we are constantly striving to unlock our full potential and achieve success in our professional lives. One of the most effective ways to do this is through self-coaching, specifically, setting and achieving goals. However, setting goals is only the first step. To truly unlock our potential and reach the pinnacle of success, we must create a strategic action plan to guide us along the way.

The first step in creating an action plan for goal achievement is to clearly define our goals. This involves setting specific, measurable, attainable, relevant, and time-bound (SMART) objectives. By clearly defining what we want to achieve, we can create a roadmap that will help us stay focused and motivated.

Once we have defined our goals, the next step is to break them down into smaller, manageable tasks. This allows us to create a step-by-step plan of action that will lead us towards our ultimate objective. By breaking our goals down into smaller tasks, we can overcome feelings of overwhelm and stay on track.

Next, it is essential to prioritize our tasks. Not all tasks are created equal, and some will have a greater impact on our goal achievement than others. By prioritizing our tasks, we can ensure that we are dedicating our time and energy to the most important activities that will propel us forward.

In addition, it is crucial to establish a timeline for completing each task. Without a deadline, tasks can easily fall by the wayside and hinder our progress. By setting deadlines for each task, we create a sense of urgency and accountability that will keep us motivated and focused.

Furthermore, it is important to regularly review and adjust our action plan as needed. The business landscape is constantly evolving, and circumstances may change. By regularly reviewing our plan, we can adapt and make necessary adjustments to ensure we are still on track towards our goals.

In conclusion, creating an action plan for goal achievement is a critical component of self-coaching for success in business leadership. By clearly defining our goals, breaking them down into smaller tasks, prioritizing those tasks, establishing timelines, and regularly reviewing and adjusting our plan, we can effectively unlock our potential and achieve the success we desire. With a well-crafted action plan, we can confidently navigate the challenges and obstacles that come our way, reaching new heights in our professional lives.

Chapter 3: Self-Assessment and Reflection for Growth

Assessing Your Strengths and Weaknesses as a Business Leader

In the fast-paced world of business leadership, it is crucial to have a clear understanding of your strengths and weaknesses. Knowing what you excel at and areas where you need improvement can significantly impact your success as a leader. In this section, we will explore the importance of self-assessment and provide practical strategies for assessing your strengths and weaknesses as a business leader.

Self-coaching for goal setting and achievement is a niche that requires a deep understanding of oneself. To unlock your potential and drive success in business leadership, it is essential to begin with an honest evaluation of your strengths. What are the skills and qualities that set you apart? Are you a natural communicator, an analytical thinker, or an exceptional analytical person? Identifying your strengths allows you to leverage them and capitalize on opportunities that align with your skillset.

Equally important is recognizing your weaknesses. It takes humility and self-awareness to acknowledge areas where you may be lacking, yet this self-assessment is crucial for personal growth and development. Are there specific skills or knowledge gaps that hold you back? Do you struggle with delegation or have difficulty managing conflict? Identifying weaknesses allows you to seek opportunities for improvement and take proactive steps to address them.

One effective strategy for assessing your strengths and weaknesses is soliciting feedback from others. Reach out to your team members, colleagues, and mentors for their input on your strengths and areas for improvement. Their perspectives can provide valuable insights that you may not have considered. Additionally, consider utilizing personality assessments or leadership evaluations to gain a more objective understanding of your strengths and weaknesses.

Once you have identified your strengths and weaknesses, develop an action plan to capitalize on your strengths and address your weaknesses. Seek out opportunities to further develop and refine your strengths, such as attending workshops or networking events focused on those areas. To overcome weaknesses, consider seeking mentorship or additional training to acquire the skills necessary for improvement.

Assessing your strengths and weaknesses as a business leader is an ongoing process. Regularly revisit your self-assessment to track your progress and adapt your action plan accordingly. By continuously investing in self-coaching for goal setting and achievement, you will unlock your potential and drive success in your business leadership journey. Remember, self-awareness is the key to unlocking your true potential as a leader.

Identifying Areas for Improvement

In the journey towards personal and professional growth, self-awareness plays a pivotal role. As business leaders, it is crucial to continuously assess our strengths and weaknesses to unlock our full potential and drive success in our organizations. This section focuses on the importance of identifying areas for improvement and provides practical strategies for self-coaching in goal setting and achievement.

Recognizing our own limitations and areas that need improvement is not a sign of weakness; rather, it is a testament to our commitment towards constant growth. By acknowledging these areas, we gain valuable insights into where we can enhance our skills, knowledge, and abilities, leading to improved performance and better leadership.

To embark on the journey of identifying areas for improvement, it is essential to adopt a growth mindset – the belief that our abilities can be developed through dedication and hard work. This mindset encourages us to view challenges as opportunities for learning and growth, rather than obstacles to overcome. By cultivating this mindset, we become more open to feedback and more willing to reflect on our actions and behaviors.

One effective strategy for identifying areas for improvement is conducting a self-assessment. This involves analyzing our strengths, weaknesses, and areas of interest. By evaluating our skills and knowledge, we can identify gaps that need to be addressed. Additionally, seeking input from trusted mentors, colleagues, or employees can provide valuable perspectives on areas that may require improvement.

Another powerful tool for self-coaching in goal setting and achievement is setting SMART (Specific, Measurable, Achievable, Relevant, and Time-bound) goals. By setting clear and specific goals, we can focus our efforts on areas that need improvement. Regularly reviewing our progress and adjusting our goals accordingly helps us stay on track and ensures continuous improvement.

Furthermore, seeking opportunities for professional development, such as attending workshops, conferences, or obtaining certifications, can provide targeted learning experiences and help bridge any skill gaps. Engaging in self-reflection exercises, journaling, or collaborating with a coach or mentor can also be beneficial in identifying areas for improvement and developing action plans to address them.

In conclusion, identifying areas for improvement is a crucial step for business leaders in unlocking their potential and achieving success. By adopting a growth mindset, conducting self-assessments, setting SMART goals, and pursuing continuous learning, leaders can continually enhance their skills and become more effective in their roles. Embracing self-coaching for goal setting and achievement empowers leaders to take ownership of their development and drive positive change within themselves and their organizations.

Reflecting on Past Experiences for Personal and Professional Growth

In the fast-paced world of business leadership, it is easy to get caught up in the hustle and bustle of day-to-day operations and forget to take a step back to reflect on our past experiences. However, reflecting on our past experiences is a crucial element for personal and professional growth. It allows us to learn from our successes and failures, gain valuable insights, and unlock our potential for success in business leadership.

Self-coaching for goal setting and achievement is a powerful tool that can help business leaders harness the benefits of reflecting on past experiences. By taking the time to review and analyze our past experiences, we can identify patterns, strengths, and areas for improvement. This self-awareness is essential for setting meaningful and achievable goals that align with our values and aspirations.

Reflecting on past experiences also provides an opportunity to celebrate our achievements. By recognizing and acknowledging our successes, we can boost our confidence and motivation, setting the stage for even greater accomplishments in the future. Additionally, reflecting on past achievements can help us identify the strategies and behaviors that led to our success, enabling us to replicate and build upon them.

On the other hand, reflecting on past failures and setbacks is equally important for personal and professional growth. It allows us to learn from our mistakes, understand what went wrong, and develop strategies to avoid similar pitfalls in the future. Embracing failure as a learning opportunity is a hallmark of successful business leaders, as it fosters resilience, adaptability, and a growth mindset.

Furthermore, reflecting on past experiences can provide valuable insights into our leadership style and its impact on others. By examining our interactions, decisions, and communication patterns, we can identify areas where we can improve our leadership skills. This self-awareness enables us to develop more effective leadership strategies, build stronger relationships with our team members, and create a positive and productive work environment.

In conclusion, reflecting on past experiences is a powerful self-coaching tool for business leaders focused on goal setting and achievement. It allows us to learn from both our successes and failures, gain valuable insights, and develop strategies for personal and professional growth. By taking the time to reflect on our past experiences, we can unlock our potential, enhance our leadership skills, and achieve success in the dynamic world of business leadership.

Chapter 4: Developing Effective Leadership Skills through Self-Coaching

Communication Skills for Effective Leadership

In today's fast-paced and interconnected business world, effective communication is the cornerstone of successful leadership. As a business leader, your ability to communicate clearly, confidently, and compassionately can make all the difference in achieving your goals and driving your team towards success. This section will explore the essential communication skills that every leader should possess, offering practical techniques and strategies for improving your communication prowess.

One of the fundamental aspects of effective communication is active listening. By truly hearing and understanding others, you can foster a culture of trust, empathy, and collaboration within your organization. This section will delve into the art of active listening, providing guidance on how to be fully present, ask thoughtful questions, and demonstrate genuine interest in others' perspectives.

Furthermore, mastering the art of persuasion is paramount for any leader. The ability to influence and inspire others is crucial for achieving your vision and garnering support from your team. In this section, you will learn various persuasive techniques, such as storytelling, using compelling data, and appealing to emotions. By honing these skills, you can motivate your team, gain buy-in for your ideas, and create a shared sense of purpose.

Another vital communication skill for effective leadership is the art of giving and receiving feedback. Constructive feedback is essential for personal and professional growth but delivering it in a way that inspires growth and improvement is an art form. This section will explore strategies for providing feedback that is specific, actionable, and delivered with empathy and respect. Additionally, you will learn how to receive feedback gracefully, utilizing it as a tool for self-improvement and fostering a culture of continuous learning within your organization.

Finally, effective leadership communication also involves the ability to adapt your communication style to different individuals and situations. This section will provide insights into various communication styles and offer practical tips on tailoring your message to different audiences, whether it be your team, clients, or stakeholders. By understanding the diverse needs and preferences of those you interact with, you can build stronger relationships and achieve greater success in your leadership role.

In conclusion, communication skills are vital for effective leadership. By actively listening, mastering the art of persuasion, giving, and receiving feedback, and adapting your communication style, you can unlock your potential as a business leader. This section will equip you with the necessary tools and strategies to enhance your communication skills, enabling you to inspire, motivate, and lead your team towards success.

Building and Leading High-Performing Teams

In today's competitive business landscape, the ability to build and lead high-performing teams is essential for success. Great leaders understand that the collective power of a team far exceeds the capabilities of any individual. This section will provide valuable insights and strategies for business leaders who are looking to unlock the potential of their teams and achieve remarkable results.

To build a high-performing team, it is crucial to focus on selecting the right individuals. Look for individuals who not only possess the necessary skills and qualifications but also align with the values and culture of your organization. Diversity of thought and background can bring fresh perspectives and innovative ideas to the table, fostering creativity and problem-solving.

Once the team is assembled, effective leadership becomes paramount. A leader's role is to create a supportive and empowering environment where team members feel valued, motivated, and encouraged to contribute their best. This can be achieved through clear communication, active listening, and providing timely feedback. Effective leaders also delegate tasks based on individual strengths, fostering a sense of ownership and accountability.

High-performing teams thrive on trust and collaboration. Encourage open and honest communication, promote healthy debate, and create opportunities for team members to work together towards common goals. Foster a culture of continuous learning and development, where team members can acquire new skills and knowledge, enabling them to perform at their best.

Recognizing and celebrating achievements is another crucial aspect of leading high-performing teams. Acknowledge and reward individual and team successes, reinforcing a positive and supportive work environment. Encourage a growth mindset, where failures are seen as opportunities for learning and improvement.

To self-coach for goal setting and achievement, business leaders must also set clear goals for their teams and provide the necessary resources and support to achieve them. Regularly assess progress, adjust as needed, and provide guidance and mentorship to help team members overcome obstacles. By setting high expectations and inspiring a shared vision, leaders can motivate their teams to reach new heights of performance.

In conclusion, building and leading high-performing teams is a critical skill for business leaders. By selecting the right individuals, fostering a supportive environment, promoting collaboration, recognizing achievements, and setting clear goals, leaders can unlock the potential of their teams and achieve remarkable success in today's competitive business world.

Emotional Intelligence and Self-Awareness in Business Leadership

In the fast-paced and competitive world of business leadership, success is not solely determined by technical skills or strategic planning. It is also heavily influenced by emotional intelligence and self-awareness. These two qualities are essential for effective decision-making, building strong relationships, and nurturing a positive work culture. In this section, we will explore the significance of emotional intelligence and self-awareness, and how they can be harnessed for success in business leadership.

Emotional intelligence refers to the ability to recognize, understand, and manage one's own emotions as well as the emotions of others. It involves empathy, self-regulation, motivation, social skills, and self-awareness. Business leaders with high emotional intelligence are adept at understanding the needs, concerns, and motivations of their team members, clients, and stakeholders. They can effectively communicate, resolve conflicts, and inspire others to achieve their full potential.

Self-awareness, on the other hand, is the foundation of emotional intelligence. It involves being in tune with one's own emotions, strengths, weaknesses, values, and blind spots. Business leaders who possess self-awareness have a clear understanding of their impact on others and are open to feedback. This allows them to make better decisions, adapt to changing circumstances, and continuously improve their leadership style.

In the realm of self-coaching for goal setting and achievement, emotional intelligence and self-awareness play a crucial role. By developing these qualities, business leaders can set meaningful goals that align with their personal values and the needs of their organization. They can also navigate challenges and setbacks with resilience, as they have a deep understanding of their emotions and triggers.

Furthermore, emotional intelligence and self-awareness enable business leaders to build and maintain strong relationships. They can establish trust, inspire loyalty, and foster a collaborative work environment. This not only enhances productivity and innovation but also creates a positive organizational culture that attracts and retains top talent.

To cultivate emotional intelligence and self-awareness, business leaders can engage in various self-coaching practices. These may include mindfulness exercises, journaling, reflection, seeking feedback, and ongoing personal development. By dedicating time and effort to self-coaching, leaders can unlock their full potential and become more effective in achieving their goals.

In conclusion, emotional intelligence and self-awareness are essential qualities for business leaders seeking success in today's dynamic and competitive environment. By honing these skills through self-coaching, leaders can make better decisions, build strong relationships, and create a positive work culture. Unlocking your potential as a business leader requires a deep understanding of yourself and others – and that begins with emotional intelligence and self-awareness.

Chapter 5: Overcoming Obstacles and Building Resilience

Understanding and Managing Stress in Business Leadership

In today's fast-paced and competitive business world, stress has become an ever-present reality for business leaders. The pressures of meeting targets, making critical decisions, and managing a team can often lead to overwhelming stress. However, it is crucial for business leaders to understand and manage stress effectively to ensure their own well-being and the success of their organizations. This section aims to provide valuable insights and strategies for understanding and managing stress in business leadership.

Firstly, it is essential to understand the nature of stress and its impact on our physical and mental well-being. Stress is a natural response to demanding situations, but when it becomes chronic, it can lead to burnout, decreased productivity, and even health issues. By recognizing the signs and symptoms of stress, business leaders can take proactive measures to address it before it escalates.

Next, this section explores various techniques for managing stress in business leadership. One effective approach is to develop a dedicated support system, whether through mentoring, networking, or seeking professional guidance. Surrounding oneself with trusted advisors and peers can provide valuable insights and emotional support during challenging times.

Additionally, self-coaching for goal setting and achievement can be a powerful tool in stress management. By setting realistic goals, breaking them down into manageable tasks, and tracking progress, business leaders can regain a sense of control and reduce stress levels. Moreover, cultivating a growth mindset and embracing resilience can help leaders navigate setbacks and challenges effectively.

Furthermore, this section delves into the importance of self-care in stress management. Business leaders often neglect their own well-being while focusing on organizational success. However, prioritizing self-care activities such as exercise, mindfulness, and leisure time is essential for recharging and maintaining optimal performance. It is crucial for business leaders to recognize that taking care of themselves is not a luxury but a necessity.

Lastly, this section emphasizes the significance of creating a positive and supportive organizational culture to mitigate stress. By fostering open communication, providing resources for stress management, and promoting work-life balance, business leaders can create an environment that supports employee well-being and reduces overall stress levels.

In conclusion, understanding and managing stress in business leadership is vital for the success and well-being of both leaders and organizations. By recognizing the impact of stress, implementing effective strategies, and promoting a supportive culture, business leaders can navigate the challenges of the modern business world while maintaining their own resilience and achieving long-term success.

Developing Resilience to Navigate Challenges

In today's fast-paced and ever-changing business landscape, challenges and obstacles are inevitable. As a business leader, one must possess the ability to adapt and navigate through these challenges effectively. This section aims to provide valuable insights and strategies for developing resilience, a crucial skill that can help propel your success in business leadership.

Resilience is the capacity to bounce back from setbacks, overcome adversity, and maintain a positive mindset in the face of challenges. It is a skill that can be developed and honed through self-coaching techniques for goal setting and achievement. By mastering resilience, you can transform setbacks into opportunities for growth and success.

The first step towards developing resilience is embracing a growth mindset. This mindset acknowledges that failures and setbacks are part of the journey to success. By reframing setbacks as learning experiences, you can develop the resilience needed to overcome future challenges. Self-coaching exercises, such as journaling and positive affirmations, can help cultivate a growth mindset and build resilience.

Another crucial aspect of developing resilience is the ability to manage stress and emotions effectively. Business leaders often face high-pressure situations that can take a toll on their mental and emotional well-being. Self-coaching techniques such as deep breathing exercises, mindfulness, and meditation can help reduce stress levels and enhance emotional resilience. By developing emotional intelligence, you can better navigate challenging situations and make informed decisions.

Furthermore, building a dedicated support network is essential for developing resilience. Surrounding yourself with like-minded individuals who can offer support, guidance, and constructive feedback can significantly contribute to your ability to overcome challenges. Self-coaching exercises such as networking, mentoring, and seeking peer support can help you build a robust support system that will assist you in navigating through challenging times.

Lastly, resilience is linked to maintaining a healthy work-life balance. Business leaders often find themselves overwhelmed with work commitments, leaving little time for personal well-being. Self-coaching techniques such as time management, prioritization, and setting boundaries can help you strike a healthy balance between work and personal life. By taking care of your physical and mental well-being, you can build the resilience necessary to face challenges head-on.

In conclusion, developing resilience is crucial for business leaders to navigate through challenges successfully. By embracing a growth mindset, managing stress and emotions effectively, building a dedicated support network, and maintaining a healthy work-life balance, you can cultivate resilience and unlock your potential for success in business leadership. Through self-coaching techniques for goal setting and achievement, you can develop the mindset and skills necessary to overcome obstacles, turning them into opportunities for growth and achievement.

Overcoming Self-Doubt and Building Confidence as a Business Leader

In the fast-paced and competitive world of business leadership, self-doubt can often creep in and hinder our progress. The ability to overcome self-doubt and build confidence is crucial for achieving success in any professional endeavor. This section aims to provide business leaders with practical strategies and self-coaching techniques to conquer self-doubt and cultivate unwavering confidence.

Self-doubt is a common experience shared by many business leaders. It can stem from a fear of failure, imposter syndrome, or a lack of belief in one's abilities. However, it is important to recognize that self-doubt is just a perception and not an accurate reflection of our true potential. By understanding this, we can start the journey towards overcoming self-doubt.

The first step in conquering self-doubt is to identify and challenge our negative self-talk. Often, we engage in negative self-talk without even realizing it.

By becoming aware of our inner dialogue, we can start to replace negative thoughts with positive affirmations. Self-coaching exercises such as daily affirmations and visualization can be incredibly powerful tools in reprogramming our mindset and building self-confidence.

Another effective strategy for overcoming self-doubt is to celebrate our successes, no matter how small they may seem. Often, we tend to downplay our achievements, focusing instead on our perceived failures. By acknowledging and celebrating even the smallest wins, we can boost our confidence and remind ourselves of our capabilities.

Building a support network of like-minded individuals is also essential in overcoming self-doubt. Surrounding ourselves with positive and supportive people who believe in our abilities can have a profound impact on our confidence levels. Networking events, mentorship programs, and joining professional organizations are great ways to connect with fellow business leaders who can offer guidance and encouragement.

Finally, it is important to remember that confidence is a skill that can be developed and strengthened over time. By stepping outside of our comfort zones and taking calculated risks, we can expand our capabilities and prove to ourselves that we can achieve important things.

In conclusion, self-doubt is a common obstacle faced by business leaders, but it can be overcome with the right mindset and strategies. By challenging negative self-talk, celebrating successes, building a support network, and taking calculated risks, business leaders can cultivate unwavering confidence and unlock their true potential. The journey to overcoming self-doubt may not be easy, but the rewards are immeasurable – a leader who is confident, resilient, and capable of achieving extraordinary success.

Chapter 6: Cultivating a Growth Mindset for Business Success

Embracing a Growth Mindset for Continuous Learning and Improvement

In today's fast-paced and ever-evolving business landscape, the ability to adapt and grow is crucial for success. As business leaders, it is essential to cultivate a growth mindset that allows for continuous learning and improvement. This section aims to provide insights and strategies to help you embrace this mindset, enabling you to excel in your self-coaching journey for goal setting and achievement.

A growth mindset is the belief that one's abilities and intelligence can be developed through dedication and hard work. On the other hand, a fixed mindset assumes that intelligence and abilities are fixed traits, limiting one's potential for growth. By adopting a growth mindset, business leaders can open themselves up to new possibilities, challenge their existing beliefs, and embrace the journey of self-improvement.

The first step in embracing a growth mindset is to develop a passion for learning. As a business leader, it is essential to be curious and open-minded, constantly seeking new knowledge and skills. Embrace challenges as opportunities for growth and view setbacks as learning experiences rather than failures. By reframing these experiences, you can extract valuable lessons and apply them to future endeavors.

Another crucial aspect of a growth mindset is the understanding that effort and persistence lead to mastery. Set realistic goals for yourself and your team and break them down into manageable steps. Celebrate small wins along the way, as they serve as motivation and reinforce the belief that progress is possible through consistent effort.

Additionally, surround yourself with a supportive network of mentors, coaches, and like-minded individuals who can provide guidance and encouragement. Collaborate with others, share knowledge, and engage in constructive feedback. By embracing diverse perspectives, you can gain new insights and expand your horizons.

Lastly, remember that failures are an inevitable part of growth. Instead of shying away from them, view failures as steppingstones to success. Analyze what went wrong, identify areas for improvement, and adjust your strategies accordingly. Embracing a growth mindset means embracing the process of trial and error, understanding that each setback brings you closer to achieving your goals.

In conclusion, adopting a growth mindset is crucial for business leaders seeking continuous learning and improvement. By developing a passion for learning, embracing challenges, persisting through obstacles, nurturing a supportive network, and reframing failures, you can unlock your potential and achieve success in your self-coaching journey for goal setting and achievement. Embrace the journey, and watch your skills, knowledge, and leadership abilities flourish.

Developing a Positive and Solution-Oriented Attitude

In the fast-paced and ever-changing world of business leadership, having a positive and solution-oriented attitude is essential for success. It is the cornerstone of self-coaching for goal setting and achievement. This section will delve into the importance of cultivating such an attitude and provide practical tips on how to develop and maintain it.

A positive attitude is not just about being optimistic or cheerful; it goes beyond that. It is about approaching challenges and setbacks with a mindset focused on finding solutions rather than dwelling on problems. Business leaders who possess a positive attitude are more resilient, adaptable, and better equipped to manage the pressures and uncertainties of the corporate world.

One way to develop a positive and solution-oriented attitude is by reframing negative situations. Instead of viewing setbacks as failures, see them as opportunities for growth and learning. By shifting your perspective, you can uncover valuable lessons and insights that will propel you forward.

Another key aspect is self-awareness. Recognize your own strengths and weaknesses and be honest with yourself about areas that need improvement. A positive attitude means embracing challenges as opportunities to develop new skills and expand your knowledge base. Seek feedback from trusted mentors or colleagues to gain insights into areas for improvement.

Practicing gratitude is also instrumental in developing a cheerful outlook. Take time each day to acknowledge and appreciate the things that are going well in your professional and personal life. This will help shift your focus from problems to possibilities, fostering a more optimistic outlook.

Engaging in positive self-talk is another powerful tool. Replace negative thoughts and self-doubt with affirmations and encouraging statements. Remind yourself of past achievements and successes, reinforcing your ability to overcome obstacles and achieve your goals.

Furthermore, surround yourself with positive and like-minded individuals. Seek networking opportunities, join professional organizations, or form mastermind groups to connect with people who share your values and aspirations. Their positive energy and support will contribute to your overall attitude and motivation.

In conclusion, developing a positive and solution-oriented attitude is crucial for business leaders seeking self-coaching for goal setting and achievement. It empowers you to overcome challenges, adapt to change, and maintain a resilient mindset. By reframing negative situations, practicing gratitude, engaging in positive self-talk, and surrounding yourself with positive individuals, you will cultivate an attitude that drives success in both your personal and professional life.

Embracing Change and Adaptability in Business Leadership

In today's rapidly evolving business landscape, change is not merely a possibility; it is a constant. As business leaders, it is crucial that we embrace change and develop a mindset of adaptability to thrive in this dynamic environment. This section aims to provide you, esteemed business leaders, with insights and strategies to navigate change successfully and cultivate adaptability within yourself and your teams.

Change, although often met with resistance and fear, presents numerous opportunities for growth and innovation. By embracing change, you can stay ahead of the curve and gain a competitive edge in your industry. However, to do so effectively, it is essential to develop a solid foundation of self-coaching for goal setting and achievement.

One key aspect of embracing change is fostering a growth mindset. This mindset allows you to view challenges as opportunities for personal and professional development. By shifting your perspective, you can approach change with curiosity and excitement, rather than fear and uncertainty. This mindset will enable you to adapt quickly and seize the opportunities that change brings.

Another crucial element of embracing change is cultivating a culture of continuous learning within your organization. Encouraging your team members to constantly seek new knowledge and skills will empower them to adapt and thrive in a rapidly changing environment. As a leader, you must lead by example and demonstrate a commitment to lifelong learning. By doing so, you will create a culture that embraces change and fosters innovation.

Furthermore, effective communication is paramount when navigating change. Open and transparent communication channels will help your team members understand the reasons behind the change and alleviate any anxieties they may have. By keeping everyone well-informed, you can foster a sense of trust and collaboration, enabling your team to embrace change and adapt collectively.

Lastly, it is crucial to develop resilience as a leader. Change often brings unforeseen challenges and setbacks, but by cultivating resilience, you can bounce back stronger and help your team do the same. Resilience allows you to maintain a positive mindset, persevere through adversity, and inspire your team during times of change.

In conclusion, embracing change and developing adaptability is essential for success in today's business environment. By cultivating a growth mindset, fostering a culture of continuous learning, promoting effective communication, and developing resilience, you can position yourself and your organization as leaders in your industry. Remember, change is not a threat; it is an opportunity. Embrace it, adapt to it, and unlock your potential for success in business leadership.

Chapter 7: Effective Time Management and Productivity Strategies

Prioritizing Tasks and Managing Time Effectively

In today's fast-paced business world, time is a valuable resource that must be managed effectively to achieve success in business leadership. As a business leader, it is crucial to prioritize tasks and optimize time management skills to maximize productivity and reach your goals. This section will provide you with effective strategies to prioritize tasks and manage your time efficiently, empowering you to unlock your potential for success.

One of the first steps in effectively prioritizing tasks is to establish clear goals. By setting specific, measurable, attainable, relevant, and time-bound (SMART) goals, you can gain clarity on what needs to be accomplished and prioritize tasks accordingly. Understanding the significance of each task in relation to your goals will enable you to prioritize effectively.

To further enhance your time management skills, it is essential to identify and eliminate time-wasting activities. Analyze your daily routine and identify any activities that do not contribute significantly to your goals or bring value to your work. By eliminating or delegating these non-essential tasks, you can free up time for activities that drive your business forward.

Another valuable technique for effective time management is the Eisenhower Matrix. This matrix categorizes tasks into four quadrants based on their urgency and importance. By classifying tasks as urgent and important, important but not urgent, urgent but not important, or neither urgent nor important, you can prioritize your tasks accordingly. The Eisenhower Matrix helps you focus on high-priority tasks while minimizing time spent on low-value activities.

Additionally, incorporating time-blocking techniques can significantly enhance your productivity. Time-blocking involves setting aside specific blocks of time for different tasks or activities. By allocating dedicated time slots for focused work, meetings, and breaks, you can maintain a structured schedule and avoid multitasking, which often leads to decreased productivity.

Lastly, effective communication and delegation play a vital role in managing time efficiently. As a business leader, it is essential to delegate tasks to capable team members, empowering them to take ownership and contribute to the overall success of the organization. By effectively communicating expectations and delegating tasks, you can free up time to focus on high-level strategic activities.

In conclusion, prioritizing tasks and managing time effectively are essential skills for any business leader. By setting clear goals, eliminating time-wasting activities, utilizing the Eisenhower Matrix, implementing time-blocking techniques, and practicing effective delegation and communication, you can optimize your time management skills and unlock your potential for success in business leadership. With the ability to prioritize tasks effectively, you will be well-equipped to achieve your goals and drive your organization forward.

Delegating and Empowering Others for Increased Productivity

As a business leader, one of the key aspects to unlocking your potential and achieving success is learning to delegate and empower others. Effective delegation not only lightens your workload but also allows you to focus on strategic initiatives, fostering a more productive and efficient work environment. By empowering your team members, you empower the organization, leading to greater productivity and goal achievement.

Delegating tasks and responsibilities to your team is not a sign of weakness, but rather a testament to your leadership abilities. It demonstrates your trust in their skills and capabilities, giving them the opportunity to gain experience and develop professionally. By effectively delegating, you distribute the workload evenly, allowing everyone to work on tasks aligned with their strengths, which leads to increased productivity.

However, delegation is not just about assigning tasks; it is also about empowering others to make decisions and take ownership of their work. Empowered individuals are more motivated, engaged, and committed to achieving their goals. By providing clear expectations, necessary resources, and regular feedback, you create a supportive environment where individuals can take risks, learn from their mistakes, and grow professionally.

To effectively delegate and empower others, start by identifying the strengths and skills of each team member. Assign tasks that align with their expertise, allowing them to excel and contribute to the overall success of the organization. Clearly communicate your expectations, deadlines, and desired outcomes, fostering a sense of clarity and purpose.

Regularly check in with your team members, providing constructive feedback and guidance. Recognize and celebrate their achievements, creating a positive work culture that encourages continuous improvement and innovation. By empowering individuals to make decisions, you foster a sense of ownership and accountability, leading to increased productivity and goal attainment.

In conclusion, delegating and empowering others is a crucial aspect of self-coaching for goal setting and achievement. By distributing tasks, empowering individuals, and fostering a supportive work environment, you unlock the potential of your team, leading to increased productivity and success in business leadership. Embrace the power of delegation and empower your team members to reach new heights, driving both individual and organizational growth.

Managing Distractions and Enhancing Focus in Business Leadership

In today's fast-paced and ever-connected world, distractions have become a constant challenge for business leaders. With the constant barrage of emails, meetings, notifications, and other interruptions, it can be challenging to maintain focus and productivity. However, mastering the art of managing distractions is crucial for success in business leadership.

This section aims to provide valuable insights and practical strategies to help business leaders effectively manage distractions and enhance their focus. By implementing these techniques, leaders can optimize their time, energy, and resources, leading to greater productivity and success.

The first step in managing distractions is to identify and understand the most common sources of distraction. This could include technological interruptions, such as emails and phone notifications, as well as environmental factors like noise and interruptions from colleagues. By recognizing these distractions, leaders can develop an initiative-taking approach to minimize their impact.

One effective strategy for managing distractions is setting clear boundaries and priorities. By identifying the most important tasks and allocating specific time slots for them, leaders can create a structured work environment that minimizes distractions. This could involve allocating specific times for email checking or scheduling uninterrupted blocks of time for deep work.

Another valuable technique for enhancing focus is practicing mindfulness and developing a disciplined mindset. By cultivating a habit of being present in the moment and consciously redirecting attention to the task at hand, leaders can avoid getting caught up in distractions and maintain laser-like focus. Mindfulness techniques such as deep breathing exercises and meditation can also be beneficial in sharpening focus and reducing stress.

Additionally, leaders should consider creating a conducive work environment that supports focus and minimizes distractions. This could involve minimizing noise levels, establishing designated quiet areas, and providing employees with the necessary tools and resources to optimize their focus.

In conclusion, managing distractions and enhancing focus is essential for business leaders seeking success in today's fast-paced world. By understanding the sources of distraction, setting clear priorities, practicing mindfulness, and creating a supportive work environment, leaders can optimize their focus and productivity. By implementing these strategies, business leaders can unlock their potential and achieve their goals, leading to greater success in their leadership endeavors.

Chapter 8: Nurturing Work-Life Balance and Well-being

Balancing Work and Personal Life as a Business Leader

As a business leader, achieving success in your professional life is undoubtedly important. However, it is equally crucial to find a balance between work and personal life to ensure overall well-being and long-term success. This section will explore effective strategies for maintaining this balance and provide self-coaching tools for goal setting and achievement in both areas.

Work-life balance is a delicate equilibrium that requires intentional effort and self-awareness. It is essential to prioritize personal well-being and invest time and energy into activities outside of work. This not only promotes a healthier lifestyle but also enhances productivity and creativity when you are back in the professional setting.

One crucial aspect of achieving work-life balance is effective time management. As a business leader, it is vital to set clear boundaries and establish designated times for work and personal activities. By creating a schedule that allows for both work-related tasks and personal commitments, you can ensure that neither area of your life is neglected.

Additionally, self-coaching for goal setting and achievement plays a significant role in maintaining work-life balance. By setting realistic and attainable goals in both your professional and personal life, you can ensure that you are making progress in all areas. Self-coaching techniques, such as visualization, positive affirmations, and accountability, can help you stay focused and motivated.

Furthermore, it is important to delegate tasks and learn to trust your team. As a business leader, it can be tempting to take on all responsibilities yourself. However, by empowering your team and trusting their abilities, you can free up time for personal pursuits while still ensuring the success of your organization.

Another crucial aspect of work-life balance is self-care. Taking care of your physical, mental, and emotional well-being is essential for long-term success. Engaging in activities that bring you joy and relaxation, such as exercise, hobbies, or spending time with loved ones, can help reduce stress and promote a healthy work-life balance.

In conclusion, finding a balance between work and personal life is paramount for business leaders. By implementing effective time management strategies, setting realistic goals, delegating tasks, and prioritizing self-care, you can achieve success in both your professional and personal endeavors. Remember, work-life balance is not a one-time achievement but an ongoing process that requires consistent effort and self-reflection.

Strategies for Stress Management and Self-Care

In the fast-paced world of business leadership, stress and burnout are usual challenges that can hinder your potential for success. As a business leader, it is crucial to prioritize your well-being and practice effective stress management techniques. This section will explore strategies for stress management and self-care, empowering you to unlock your potential and achieve your goals.

One of the first steps in managing stress is recognizing the signs and symptoms. Stress can manifest in numerous ways, including physical symptoms like headaches or fatigue, as well as emotional symptoms such as irritability or anxiety. By identifying these signs, you can take initiative-taking steps to address and mitigate stress before it escalates.

One effective strategy for stress management is practicing mindfulness and relaxation techniques. Taking time for yourself each day to engage in activities like meditation, deep breathing exercises, or yoga can help you quiet your mind and reduce stress levels. These practices promote self-awareness, allowing you to better understand your own needs and manage stress effectively.

Another important aspect of stress management is creating a healthy work-life balance. As a business leader, it can be easy to prioritize work over personal life, but neglecting self-care can lead to burnout and diminished productivity. Set clear boundaries between work and personal time, and make sure to allocate time for activities that bring you joy and rejuvenation.

Additionally, building a support system is crucial for stress management. Surround yourself with individuals who offer encouragement, guidance, and understanding. Seek out mentors or coaches who can provide valuable insights and help you navigate the challenges of leadership. Remember, you do not have to face stress alone.

Furthermore, self-care extends beyond stress management. It involves nurturing your physical, emotional, and mental well-being. Prioritize regular exercise, a balanced diet, and sufficient sleep to maintain optimal physical health. Engage in activities that bring you joy and fulfillment, whether it is spending time with loved ones, pursuing a hobby, or simply enjoying nature.

By implementing these strategies for stress management and self-care, you will be better equipped to manage the demands of business leadership. Remember, self-coaching for goal setting and achievement requires a solid foundation of self-care and stress management. Prioritize your well-being and unlock your potential for success in both your professional and personal life.

Cultivating a Healthy and Supportive Work Environment

A healthy and supportive work environment is the foundation of success in any business. It not only enhances employee well-being but also fosters productivity, creativity, and innovation. As a business leader, it is crucial to understand the importance of creating and maintaining such an environment to unlock the full potential of your team. In this section, we will explore the key strategies for cultivating a healthy and supportive work environment, providing you with the tools to become a self-coaching expert in goal setting and achievement.

First, effective communication is the cornerstone of a healthy work environment. Encourage open and honest dialogue between team members, ensuring that everyone feels heard and valued. Create a culture of respect, where ideas and opinions are welcomed, and constructive feedback is given and received in a constructive manner. By fostering a communication-rich environment, you can build trust among team members and promote collaboration, enabling the achievement of shared goals.

Another vital aspect of a healthy work environment is promoting work-life balance. Encourage your team to prioritize self-care and maintain a healthy equilibrium between work and personal life. Provide flexible working arrangements whenever possible, allowing employees to manage their time effectively and reduce stress. By demonstrating that you value their well-being, you will create a supportive atmosphere where individuals feel motivated and inspired to succeed.

Furthermore, cultivating a culture of continuous learning and professional growth is essential for creating a healthy work environment. Encourage employees to pursue personal development opportunities, such as workshops, seminars, and online courses. Provide regular training sessions and mentorship programs to enhance their skills and knowledge. By investing in your team's growth, you not only empower them to reach their full potential but also foster a sense of loyalty and commitment to the organization.

Lastly, recognize and reward achievements within your team. Celebrate both individual and collective successes, acknowledging the hard work and dedication of your employees. This not only boosts morale but also creates a positive and motivating work environment. By fostering a culture of appreciation, you inspire your team to strive for excellence and continuously improve.

In conclusion, cultivating a healthy and supportive work environment is crucial for business leaders seeking self-coaching for goal setting and achievement. By prioritizing effective communication, work-life balance, continuous learning, and recognition of achievements, you can unlock the full potential of your team. Remember, a healthy work environment is the bedrock upon which success is built, enabling individuals to thrive and businesses to flourish.

Chapter 9: Building and Sustaining Motivation for Business Success

Discovering and Aligning with Personal and Professional Values

In today's fast-paced and competitive business world, it is crucial for business leaders to not only have an unobstructed vision and set goals for success but also to align those goals with their personal and professional values. This section will explore the importance of discovering and aligning personal and professional values and how it can lead to greater fulfillment and success in business leadership.

When we talk about personal values, we refer to the principles and beliefs that guide our behavior and decision-making process. They reflect what is most important to us as individuals and shape our identity. Professional values, on the other hand, are the set of ethical standards and principles that govern our behavior in the workplace. Identifying and understanding these values is essential for self-coaching in goal setting and achievement in business leadership.

Discovering personal and professional values requires self-reflection and introspection. It involves asking yourself questions like, "What do I stand for?" and "What are the principles that guide my actions?" By taking the time to reflect on these questions, business leaders can gain clarity about their core values and use them as a compass to navigate their professional journey.

Aligning personal and professional values is crucial because it ensures that business leaders are acting in congruence with their authentic selves. When our actions align with our values, we experience a sense of fulfillment and purpose that motivates us to excel in our roles. It also helps build trust and credibility with colleagues, employees, and stakeholders, as they see us leading with integrity and authenticity.

Incorporating personal and professional values into goal setting and achievement is a powerful tool for business leaders. By aligning goals with values, leaders can create a sense of meaning and purpose in their work. When our goals are in line with our values, we are more likely to stay motivated and committed, even when faced with challenges or setbacks.

To unlock your potential in business leadership, it is essential to discover and align with your personal and professional values. By understanding what truly matters to you and incorporating those values into your goals and actions, you can achieve greater success, fulfillment, and satisfaction in your professional journey. So, take the time to reflect on your values, align them with your goals, and watch as your leadership potential soars to new heights.

Setting Meaningful Goals for Long-Term Motivation

In the fast-paced world of business leadership, setting meaningful goals is essential for long-term motivation and success. As a business leader, you are constantly faced with challenges and opportunities that require you to stay focused and driven. This section will introduce you to the power of self-coaching for goal setting and achievement, providing you with practical strategies to unlock your potential and achieve your desired outcomes.

One of the first steps in setting meaningful goals is identifying your values and passions. Take the time to reflect on what truly matters to you and what drives you in your professional life. By aligning your goals with your core values, you are more likely to stay motivated and committed to their achievement. This section will guide you through a series of exercises that will help you gain clarity on your values and passions, allowing you to set goals that are meaningful and fulfilling.

Another key aspect of goal setting is ensuring that your goals are specific, measurable, attainable, relevant, and time-bound (SMART). This section will provide you with a step-by-step process to create SMART goals that are realistic and challenging enough to keep you motivated. You will learn how to break down big goals into smaller, actionable steps, making them more manageable and increasing your chances of success.

Furthermore, this section will explore the importance of visualization and positive affirmation in goal achievement. By visualizing your desired outcomes and regularly affirming your ability to achieve them, you can tap into the power of your subconscious mind and boost your motivation. You will discover practical techniques to incorporate visualization and positive affirmation into your daily routine, enhancing your focus and determination.

Additionally, this section will address the significance of tracking your progress and celebrating your achievements along the way. Regularly reviewing your goals and measuring your progress will not only keep you accountable but also provide you with a sense of accomplishment and motivation to continue pushing forward. You will learn effective strategies to track your progress and adjust your goals as needed, ensuring that you stay on the path to long-term success.

In conclusion, setting meaningful goals is crucial for long-term motivation and success in business leadership. This section will equip you with the tools and techniques of self-coaching for goal setting and achievement. By aligning your goals with your values, creating SMART goals, visualizing success, tracking progress, and celebrating achievements, you will unlock your potential and realize your full capabilities as a business leader. Get ready to embark on a transformative journey towards

achieving your goals and unlocking your true
potential!

Celebrating Milestones and Maintaining Momentum

In the fast-paced world of business leadership,
setting goals and achieving them is just the
beginning of the journey towards success. It is
crucial for business leaders to not only celebrate
milestones but also maintain the momentum to
continue moving forward. This section aims to guide
business leaders in self-coaching for goal setting and
achievement, providing insights on how to celebrate
achievements and sustain motivation.

One of the most effective ways to celebrate
milestones is by acknowledging and appreciating the
hard work and dedication that went into achieving
them. Business leaders can organize team
celebrations, such as a lunch or dinner, to recognize
the efforts of their employees and foster a positive
work environment. Additionally, recognizing
individual achievements through public praise and
rewards can boost morale and motivate employees to
strive for excellence.

Celebrating milestones also involves taking the time to reflect on the journey so far and the lessons learned along the way. By analyzing the strategies that led to success, business leaders can identify what worked and what could be improved upon in future endeavors. This reflection process is essential for personal growth and development, as it allows leaders to refine their skills and make better-informed decisions in the future.

While celebrating milestones is important, it is equally crucial for business leaders to maintain momentum and not become complacent. To do so, leaders must continue setting new goals that challenge them and their teams, ensuring that they are always striving for improvement. This section will provide tools and techniques for effective goal setting, including the SMART (Specific, Measurable, Achievable, Relevant, Time-bound) framework, to help business leaders maintain focus and drive.

Furthermore, maintaining momentum requires ongoing motivation and inspiration. Business leaders can achieve this by surrounding themselves with like-minded individuals who share their drive for success. Engaging in networking events and seeking mentorship opportunities can provide invaluable support and guidance, keeping leaders motivated and inspired throughout their journey.

In conclusion, celebrating milestones and maintaining momentum are crucial aspects of self-coaching for success in business leadership. By acknowledging achievements, reflecting on lessons learned, and setting new goals, business leaders can continuously strive for improvement and sustain their motivation. With the right strategies and mindset, leaders can unlock their full potential and achieve extraordinary success in their professional endeavors.

Chapter 10: Continuous Growth and Development as a Business Leader

Seeking Feedback and Embracing a Growth Mindset

As a business leader, it is imperative to continuously seek feedback and embrace a growth mindset to unlock your true potential and achieve success in your professional journey. This section provides valuable insights and strategies for self-coaching in goal setting and achievement, with a particular focus on seeking feedback and fostering a growth mindset.

Feedback is a powerful tool that can offer invaluable insights into your strengths, weaknesses, and areas for improvement. It provides a fresh perspective and enables you to identify blind spots that may hinder your progress. By actively seeking feedback from colleagues, mentors, and even team members, you can gain a comprehensive understanding of your performance and make necessary adjustments to enhance your leadership skills.

When seeking feedback, it is crucial to create an environment that encourages honest and constructive criticism. Foster open communication channels where individuals feel comfortable sharing their thoughts and opinions. Embrace a growth mindset by viewing feedback as an opportunity for growth rather than a personal attack. Remember, feedback is not about finding faults, but rather an opportunity to gain experience and develop.

To effectively incorporate feedback into your self-coaching process, it is essential to have a growth mindset. A growth mindset allows you to see challenges as opportunities for growth and recognize that your abilities can be developed through dedication and hard work. By embracing a growth mindset, you will be more open to receiving feedback, understanding that it is a vital part of your development journey.

In addition to seeking feedback, it is important to provide feedback to others. As a business leader, your role extends beyond personal growth; you also have the responsibility to nurture and develop your team members. By providing constructive feedback, you empower them to embrace a growth mindset and unlock their potential for success.

In conclusion, seeking feedback and embracing a growth mindset are fundamental aspects of self-coaching for goal setting and achievement. By actively seeking feedback and fostering a growth mindset, you open new possibilities for personal and professional growth. Remember that feedback is a gift that can propel you towards success, and a growth mindset is the key to unlocking your true potential. So, embrace feedback, foster a growth mindset, and watch as you soar to new heights as a business leader.

Engaging in Continuous Learning Opportunities

In today's fast-paced business world, the ability to adapt and grow is crucial for success. As a business leader, you understand the importance of constantly improving your skills and knowledge to stay ahead of the competition. This section explores the concept of engaging in continuous learning opportunities and how it can enhance your self-coaching journey for goal setting and achievement.

Continuous learning is not just about attending workshops or conferences; it is a mindset that embraces constant development and improvement. It involves seeking out new knowledge, challenging your existing beliefs, and expanding your horizons. By actively engaging in continuous learning, you can enhance your leadership skills, gain new perspectives, and unlock your true potential.

One of the key benefits of continuous learning is its impact on goal setting and achievement. As a self-coaching tool, it allows you to identify areas for improvement and set meaningful goals that align with your personal and professional aspirations. By regularly updating your skills and knowledge, you can adapt your goals to reflect the changing business landscape and stay on track towards success.

Engaging in continuous learning opportunities also provides you with a competitive advantage. In a rapidly evolving business environment, those who are willing to invest in their own development are more likely to thrive. By staying up to date with the latest industry trends and best practices, you can position yourself as a thought leader and stay ahead of the curve.

Additionally, continuous learning fosters a growth mindset, which is essential for overcoming challenges and embracing change. It encourages you to see setbacks as opportunities for learning and improvement, rather than as failures. This mindset shift can significantly impact your ability to persevere, innovate, and lead with confidence.

To engage in continuous learning, you need to be proactive and intentional. Seek out relevant books, podcasts, and online courses that align with your interests and goals. Join professional networks and attend industry events to connect with like-minded individuals and gain insights from experts. Consider finding a mentor or coach who can provide guidance and support on your self-coaching journey.

Remember, continuous learning is a lifelong process. Embrace every opportunity to expand your knowledge, challenge your assumptions, and grow as a business leader. By engaging in continuous learning, you can unlock your true potential and achieve greater success in your personal and professional life.

Creating a Personal Development Plan for Ongoing Success

In the fast-paced and competitive world of business leadership, continuous growth and development are essential for long-term success. As a business leader, it is not enough to rely solely on experience and past achievements. To stay ahead of the curve and unlock your true potential, it is vital to create a personal development plan that focuses on ongoing self-coaching for goal setting and achievement.

A personal development plan serves as a roadmap for your professional growth journey. It helps you identify your strengths, weaknesses, and areas for improvement. By setting clear goals and outlining actionable steps, you can enhance your skills, broaden your knowledge, and achieve your full potential as a business leader.

The first step in creating a personal development plan is self-reflection. Take the time to assess your current skills, knowledge, and competencies. Identify areas where you excel and those that require improvement. This self-awareness will guide you in setting realistic and meaningful goals for your development.

Next, prioritize your goals based on their relevance to your career aspirations and the needs of your business. Break them down into short-term and long-term objectives. Short-term goals can be accomplished within a few months, while long-term goals may take several years to achieve. By setting both types of goals, you create a balanced approach that ensures ongoing growth.

Once you have identified your goals, it is time to develop a plan of action. Break each goal down into smaller, manageable steps. Determine the resources and support you need to achieve them. This could include attending seminars, enrolling in courses, seeking mentorship, or networking with industry professionals. Implement a timeline and hold yourself accountable for completing each step.

Regularly review and evaluate your progress. Adjust your plan as needed, considering any changes in your goals or circumstances. Celebrate your achievements along the way to stay motivated and inspired.

Remember, self-coaching is an ongoing process. As a business leader, your personal development should be a lifelong commitment. Continuously seek new opportunities for growth, expand your knowledge, and challenge yourself to step outside your comfort zone. By investing in your personal development, you not only enhance your own skills but also inspire and motivate those around you.

Unlocking your potential as a business leader requires a personal development plan that focuses on self-coaching for goal setting and achievement. Take the first step today and embark on a journey of continuous growth and success.

Chapter 11: Conclusion

Recap of Key Concepts and Strategies

In this section, we will provide a comprehensive recap of the key concepts and strategies covered throughout this book, "Unlocking Your Potential: Self-Coaching for Success in Business Leadership." This content is specifically addressed to business leaders who are seeking self-coaching techniques for goal setting and achievement.

One of the fundamental concepts we emphasized throughout the book is the importance of self-awareness. Understanding your strengths, weaknesses, values, and motivations is essential for effective goal setting and achievement. By leveraging self-awareness, you can align your goals with your values and create a sense of purpose that drives your actions.

Another crucial concept we explored is the power of goal setting. We discussed the SMART (Specific, Measurable, Achievable, Relevant, Time-bound) framework, which helps business leaders define clear and actionable goals. Setting SMART goals allows you to focus your efforts, track progress, and make necessary adjustments along the way.

Furthermore, we delved into the significance of creating an action plan. Developing a well-structured plan is essential for turning your goals into reality. We discussed techniques such as breaking down larger goals into smaller, manageable tasks, prioritizing activities, and leveraging time management strategies to maximize productivity.

Throughout this book, we also emphasized the role of self-discipline and resilience. Achieving goals requires consistent effort, dedication, and the ability to overcome obstacles. We provided strategies for staying motivated, developing self-discipline, and cultivating a growth mindset to overcome setbacks and challenges.

Additionally, we explored the importance of effective communication and collaboration. As a business leader, you must be able to communicate your vision, delegate tasks, and build strong relationships with your team. We discussed techniques for improving communication skills, fostering teamwork, and creating a positive work environment.

Lastly, we highlighted the significance of continuous learning and personal development. As a business leader, it is crucial to stay updated with industry trends, acquire new skills, and seek opportunities for growth. We provided strategies for self-coaching, such as seeking feedback, setting learning goals, and cultivating a lifelong learning mindset.

In conclusion, this section offered a comprehensive recap of the key concepts and strategies covered in this book, "Unlocking Your Potential: Self-Coaching for Success in Business Leadership." By applying these concepts, business leaders can enhance their self-coaching abilities for goal setting and achievement, leading to greater success in their professional lives.

Final Thoughts on Self-Coaching for Success in Business Leadership

As we near the end of this book, it is crucial to reflect on the importance of self-coaching for achieving success in business leadership. Throughout these chapters, we have explored various strategies and techniques that can empower business leaders to unlock their full potential. Now, let us delve into our concluding thoughts on self-coaching for goal setting and achievement.

First, self-coaching is a powerful tool that allows business leaders to take control of their own development. It enables individuals to identify their strengths and weaknesses, set meaningful goals, and devise effective action plans. By adopting a self-coaching approach, leaders can become proactive in their personal and professional growth, rather than relying solely on external resources or guidance.

One key aspect of self-coaching is the ability to set clear and measurable goals. Successful business leaders understand the importance of setting specific, achievable objectives that are aligned with their vision and values. By breaking down larger goals into smaller, manageable steps, leaders can stay motivated and track their progress along the way.

Moreover, self-coaching encourages leaders to embrace a growth mindset. This mindset involves the belief that abilities and intelligence can be developed through dedication and hard work. By cultivating a growth mindset, business leaders can overcome challenges, learn from setbacks, and continuously improve their skills and knowledge.

In addition to goal setting and a growth mindset, self-coaching emphasizes the importance of self-reflection. Taking the time to reflect on one's actions, decisions, and outcomes can provide valuable insights for personal and professional growth. By analyzing past experiences, business leaders can identify patterns, strengths, and areas for improvement, leading to more effective leadership.

Finally, self-coaching is not a one-time endeavor but an ongoing process. Successful business leaders understand that self-coaching is a commitment to lifelong learning and development. It requires dedication, self-discipline, and a willingness to adapt and evolve. By consistently engaging in self-coaching practices, leaders can stay ahead of the curve, embrace change, and continuously strive for excellence.

In conclusion, self-coaching for success in business leadership is a transformative journey that empowers individuals to unlock their full potential. By setting clear goals, adopting a growth mindset, practicing self-reflection, and embracing lifelong learning, business leaders can navigate the complexities of leadership and achieve remarkable success. So, take charge of your own development, embrace self-coaching, and unlock your true potential as a business leader.

Act and Unlocking Your Full Potential as a Business Leader

In today's fast-paced and highly competitive business world, it is crucial for leaders to continually strive for personal growth and development. As a business leader, your ability to act and unlock your full potential plays a pivotal role in achieving success. This section aims to guide you on the path towards self-coaching for goal setting and achievement, empowering you to become the best version of yourself.

To begin with, it is important to recognize that unlocking your full potential starts with a mindset shift. Embrace the idea that you have the power to shape your own destiny and make a significant impact on your organization. Believe in yourself and your abilities and let go of any self-limiting beliefs that may be holding you back. By adopting a growth mindset, you open yourself up to endless possibilities and opportunities for growth.

Once you have the right mindset, it is time to act. Setting clear and achievable goals is the first step towards unlocking your potential. Define your long-term vision and break it down into smaller, manageable milestones. This will not only help you stay focused but also provide a sense of direction and purpose. Regularly review and adjust your goals, ensuring they align with both your personal aspirations and the needs of your organization.

To effectively achieve your goals, it is essential to develop a strategic plan. Identify the resources, skills, and support you need to succeed. Surround yourself with a network of mentors, coaches, and like-minded individuals who can provide guidance and motivation along the way. Additionally, constantly seek opportunities for learning and skill development, whether through workshops, courses, or reading relevant literature. Remember, the more you invest in yourself, the more you can bring to the table as a leader.

Lastly, be proactive in acting on your goals. Break tasks into smaller, manageable steps and prioritize them accordingly. Take calculated risks, embrace failure as a learning opportunity, and persevere in the face of challenges. Remember, true growth comes from stepping outside your comfort zone and pushing your limits.

By acting and unlocking your full potential as a business leader, you not only enhance your own success but also inspire and empower those around you. Embrace self-coaching for goal setting and achievement, and watch as you transform into a more confident, effective, and influential leader.

The Author

Jeffrey Yeomans is an accountability and Leadership Life Coach specializing in leading people. He has been supporting leadership development and daily productivity for over 24 years.

Over the last several years I have completed extensive research around business coaching and life coaching for workers. Since I started in leadership, I have noticed a definite change in leadership styles and the development of coaching and training modeled around employees.

I have worked in various industrial plants for the last 35 years. Like many people in a technical environment, I advanced up the ladder mainly because of my technical skills and my willingness to take on more responsibility. It was only after I became a supervisor that I realized I needed to improve my leadership skills.

As I searched for training material related to coaching and leadership, I came across various authors and leadership methods. I have combined all this learning and my experimentation with clients to form this self-coaching system. I designed it for people who cannot afford a professional coach.

jeffreyyeomans.com

Self-Coaching Exercises

The Self-Coaching Worksheet

The Personal Self-Coaching Exercise worksheet

This is the section of the book where you should print out the questions so that you can record your answers.

The simple questions used in this personal self-growth coaching program require that you answer them truthfully and completely to provide the results you are looking for. From experience the self-coaching model is effective in helping you obtain small to medium goals.

If you require additional assistance for larger and complex goals, then we suggest you engage a life or business coach to assist you in the full process.

Step 1:

Important goals that I want to achieve:

1._____

2._____

3._____

4._____

5._____

6. _____

Goal questions (ask Yourself for each goal above)

What are the goals I want to achieve? _____

Why am I hoping to achieve this goal? _____

Who else needs to know about the plan?
_____

How will I inform them? _____

What do I want more of in my life? _____

What would I try now if I knew I could not fail?
_____

What am I aiming for in the long/medium/short term? _____

When would I like to have reached this goal? _____

How will I know when I have achieved this goal? _____

What will it look/feel/sound like? _____

What could I do today that would make the biggest difference to my life? _____

Step 2:

Out of all goals, this one is the most important to me (complete rest of exercise with this primary goal): _____

Step 3:

Break down your goal into small actions, steps, and groups of tasks.

Step 4:

Based upon these smaller tasks, how long will it take me to achieve this goal: _____

Do I commit 100% to achieving this goal: YES____
NO____

Reward I will give to myself once I achieve this goal:

____

Reality questions (ask Yourself)

What do I see is happening now around me (this issue)?

What have I done so far towards this (goal)?
....

What is my main concern around this goal/issue?
....

What resources do I have to help me with this?
....

What might be holding me back? ....

Why haven't I reached that goal already?

....

What do I think is stopping me? _____

What do I think other people's perception of the situation is?

Do I know other people who have achieved that goal? ......

What have I already tried? _____.........

How could I turn this around this time? ....

What could I do better this time? _____

On a scale of 1-10 how severe/serious/urgent is the situation?

How is the current situation affecting me, others, my overall life? ...

What are the factors I need to consider?

....

Do I need anyone else to participate in this conversation? ...

How urgent is this situation to me? _____

How will my success/failure at addressing this affect the rest of my life or business? ....

Who else do I believe shares my concerns and needs to find a solution? ....

How will I know I have this managed? ....

Step 5:

Strengths I have that can help me to achieve this goal:

1._____

2._____

3._____

"Options" questions

What could I do to move myself one step closer to achieving my goal? ....

What are all the unusual ways I could approach this? ......

What else could I do? ....

What if I knew that I could not fail? ....

If I could think of three more things, what would they be? ...

What else could I do? What else? Anything else? What next?

What could be my first step? ....

Who else might be able to help? ....

What would happen if I did nothing? ....

What has worked for me already?

How could I do more of that? .....

What would I suggest to a friend in a comparable situation? ...

What would happen if I did that? ....

What is the hardest/most challenging part of that for me? ...

What advice would I give to a friend about that challenge?

What would I gain by doing/saying that? ....

What would I lose by doing/saying that? ....

If someone did/said that to me, what do I think would happen? ...

What is the best/worst thing about that option? ....

Which option do I feel ready to act on? Scale 1-10 what is this option? _____

"Will" questions

Which of my options feels, seems, looks, and sounds the best ...

Which would take me closer to my long-term goal? ....

Which would give me the most satisfaction? ....

On a scale of 1-10, how committed am I to this goal? ....

What would need to happen to prove I have achieved this goal?

Who do I need to talk to first? Who needs to know? ....

What would increase my success rate? (e.g., manage fear, clearer steps, more support, etc.) ....

What will happen (what is the cost) of NOT doing this? ...

How will I know if this is completed satisfactory? ....

How am I going to do this? ....

What is the first step?

When will I take the first step? ....

Could anything stop me? ....

What are the risks? ....

Step 6:

Which actions do I need to take to achieve this
goal? Analyze this goal and break it down into
smaller actionable tasks. If a goal cannot be broken
down into tasks, it is too general:

Action 1: _____.........

Action 2: _____.........

Action 3: _____.........

Action 4: _____.........

Tactic questions

How and when will I do this? ....

What is my plan to do this? ....

What support do I need to get this done? ....

What are 3 actions I can take that would make sense to do today?

What are 3 actions that I can take this week?

On a scale of 1-10, how excited do I feel about taking these actions?

What do I need from myself or others to help me achieve this?

How will I know when I have done it? ....

Who will I involve in this? ....

When will I do this? _____

Specifically what actions will I take and when will I carry them out?

What specific step will I take next?

How will that help me reach my goal?

Here are some additional tips for tactical development. You can use these tips to help give you more ideas.

Identify your Needs - Identify your needs in ways that you will understand. Create actions that will help you reach your goal.

Establish Your Success Metrics - based on growth evaluation, having a measurement for your success allows you to measure the effectiveness of your actions and plans.

Understand the Investments

PERSONAL COSTS - What will be the personal costs to these actions and changes in my life? How will I deal with both positive and negative costs that result from my actions? ....

PROCESS COSTS - What is the total cost of this process? Are the benefits I will obtain from reaching my goals and the changes made in my life worth the cost of engaging in the process? ………………

HIDDEN COSTS - Have I missed any hidden costs that I should be considering? What would I do if a cost that I was not aware of shows itself? ………………

Step 7:

Habits - Things I choose to start doing and stop doing which will help me achieve my goal:

START DOING

1. ………………………

2. …………………….

3. …………………….

4. ……………………

5. …………………….

STOP DOING

1. ....

2. ....

3. ....

4. ....

5. ....

Habit Questions

What are some good habits that I already have that can help you reach your goal? ....

What habits do you need to change to obtain your goal? ...

What is your plan to sustain your success? ....

Can you break this plan down into manageable steps? ......

Can you sustain each of these steps until they become an involuntary activity (30 days)?
....

What activities are you going to have to give up allowing for the new habit to be developed? ....

Are you committed to changing the habit?

Will you tell others about the new habit you are trying to form and why you are doing it? ....

Can you develop an affirmation around this habit to remind yourself of its importance to your success? ....

Step 8:

Which new skills/knowledge will help me achieve my goal?

1._____

2._____

3._____

4._____

5._____

When you are looking at a new habit or action, do not be afraid of taking that first step. Ask yourself; "what is the worst thing that could happen" for each action that you are nervous about or reluctant to take. Then proceed to answer that question for each action.

After you have thought about the worst thing that could happen, flip that question on its lid and ask yourself "what is the best thing that could happen" if I take this action.

Get into a habit of flipping any negative thinking into positive thinking when looking at your actions. There is always good and bad in everything we do, so if you focus on the positive outcome of the action, you are more likely to take that step towards your goal.

The actual worst thing that can happen is never as bad as you think when you really analyze it. There are very few actions for improving your life that will cause you serious physical or mental harm.

We may think an action is risky but when we really look at it objectively, a lot of reluctance is just in our mind. Change is never easy, but if you can work through those negative thoughts, you are well on your way towards your goal.

Step 9: My progress:

What is working well (accomplishments)

- ....

- ....

- ....

- ....

- ....

What do I need to change (improve)

- ....

- ....

- ....

- ....

- ....

Step 10:

Who can help me achieve this goal faster?

When you have finished this complete self-coaching exercise, you will have determined your primary goal and a process to bring it to completion. The results you can get from following this self-directed coaching model will be equal to the effort you put into following the process.

Many people have used this same process to bring about life-changing growth in their life. Whether your personal life goal is losing weight or finding a new career, the process will be the same. This is also true for business related goals.

As stated above this Personal Self Growth Results Coaching exercise is suitable for small to medium sized goals.

When you are self-coaching, it is best to focus on one goal or result at a time.

If you have a more complex goal that requires completing multiple steps you may want to consider using a personal life coach. A life coach is trained in helping people get the best results for larger projects.